QUESTIONNAIRE

To Tutors:

Read On! II is a revision of the original *Read On!* series (1978). The new edition is based on comments from users of the series and on new insights in the teaching of reading and writing.

LVA has a policy of soliciting comments from the people who actually use our materials. We use these comments in the revisions of our materials to make them even more effective. Therefore, we are especially interested in your answers to the following questions for future revisions.

1. Did you have literacy tutor training prior to using *Read On! II*? Literacy Volunteers of America _____ Laubach Literacy Action_____ Other_____ (name)_____

2. Have you used the 1978 *Read On!* series? Yes_____ No_____

3. Did you use *Read On! II* in one-to-one teaching_____ ABE drop-in_____ small groups_____ classroom_____?

4. Did you use *Read On! II* with school tutoring_____ ABE_____ library-literacy program_____ volunteer literacy program_____ other_____?

5. Did you use *Read On! II* with basic reading learner(s)_____ or English Second Language learner(s)_____ both_____?

6. What was the level of the learner(s) reading *Read On! II*?
   _____

7. What test did you use to establish the level(s)? _____
   _____

8. Was the amount of directions in *Read On ! II* too little_____ about right_____ too detailed_____ I already knew the procedure_____

9. Did the scripting in the first lesson of the book help? a lot_____ somewhat____ not at all____ I already knew the procedure____

10. What changes in the directions/scripting/stories, if any, would you suggest? _____
    _____

11. Did you teach more than one unit per lesson? one unit_____ more_____ how many more_____

12. Did you use *Read On! II* as the whole lesson____ or as a part____?

13. Were the "Suggested Activities" useful? Yes_____ No_____

14. Can you suggest other activities for inclusion in the future?

_____

_____

15. Did you use the workbooks as integrated activities with the lesson?
always_____ some of the time_____ never_____

16. What features did you feel were most helpful in *Read On! II* series?

_____

_____

_____

What features did you feel were least helpful?

_____

_____

What features would you change?

_____

_____

To Learners:

1. Did you enjoy reading the stories in Book Five of *Read On! II*
Yes_____ No_____

2. What story did you like best? _____

_____

What story did you like least? _____

_____

3. Did you use the Workbooks: with tutor_____ on my own_____
not at all _____.

4. Did you enjoy the workbook activities? Yes _____ No_____
some of them _____

5. Which kind of workbook activity did you like most? _____

_____

6. Which kind of workbook activity did you like least? _____

_____

7. What other kinds of stories would you like to read?

_____

Program Name and Address: _____

_____

Mail to: Virginia K. Lawson, Ph.D., VP Publishing/Marketing
Literacy Volunteers of America, Inc.
5795 Widewaters Parkway, Syracuse, NY 13214

Read On! II
A Sequential Reading Series
Book Five
Let Me Tell You A Story

Artis Lee, Author

V.K. Lawson, Ph.D.
Educational Designer
Project Director

Read On! II Advisory Committee

Rosemary Adams, Ph.D.
Adult Basic Education
Regional Coordinator, GA

Roy Bartoo, Ph.D.
Professor of Reading
SUNY Oneonta, NY

Ruth Colvin
LVA Founder

Janice Cuddahee
LVA New York State

Anne DuPrey
LVA Nassau County, NY

Pat Kardash
LVA Oswego, NY

Karen Kern
Laura Wilcox
Garnet Career Center, WV

Kathy Kuy
International
Institute of Boston, MA

Lester Laminack, Ed.D.
Director, Reading Center
Western Carolina University, NC

Jerri Lee
LVA Connecticut

Jolene Olson
LV of Northern Wyoming

Sue Rider
LVA Stamford, CT

Jane Root, Ph.D.
Johnson State, VT
(retired)

Susan Mandel Glazer, Ed.D. Reading Clinic, Rider College
LVA Reading Consultant

Jim Marks, Illustrator

LITERACY
VOLUNTEERS
of
AMERICA Inc.

ACKNOWLEDGEMENTS

The *Read On! II* series uses the concept of Assisted Reading. That concept and the format of tutor directions on the textbook left hand page and learner reading material on the right-hand, were developed in the original *Read On!* (1978) series by Jane Root, Ph.D. Dr. Root's presentation allowed for beginning readers to read with their tutors from the earliest lessons.

Since the original publication of *Read On!* in 1978, thousands of literacy students, tutors and trainers, as well as remedial reading teachers and learners, have used the series. Many of them have shared their thoughts and comments with us. For those comments, we are very grateful.

The *Read On! II* series is based on the advances made in the fields of reading and adult learning theory which have taken place in the nine years since the first *Read On!* was produced and on the comments of those who have used it over the years.

Much editorial and production detail work goes into developing a series of six textbooks, six workbooks, an *Instructor's Guide*, placement test and a set of *Tutor Resource Sheets.* I would like to thank not only the advisors and consultants listed on the title page of this series but also LVA national staff: Chip Carlin, Jinx Crouch, Jonathan McKallip, Margaret Price, Karen Alexander, Michelle Peterson, Jackie Iannotti, with special thanks to Barbara Jean MacDonald and Artis Lee.

V.K. Lawson, Ph.D.

The development and production of *Read On! II* was made possible with a grant from the GTE Foundation, Stamford, Ct.

All proceeds from the sale of this book go to further the work of Literacy Volunteers of America, Inc.

Let Me Tell You a Story

Table of Contents

General Principles

Read On! II is a sequential reading series which makes use of the principles of modeling and assisted reading. The approach is that of modified language experience using sight words and context clues and incorporating the decoding skills of phonics and word patterns.

If you are unfamiliar with these approaches, reading *TUTOR* (Colvin, Root, 1987) and *Tutoring Small Groups: Basic Reading,* (Ottoson, et al., 1985) will be helpful. Also, the *Read On! II Instructor's Guide* (Lawson, 1987) which accompanies the series explains these concepts in detail. The texts and workbooks contain step-by-step directions for teaching the lesson material. They also offer suggestions for alternative approaches.

A placement test is included in the *Instructor's Guide* which will help you find an appropriate starting book for learners so that a learner need not repeat material which is already known.

Directions are given in the *Instructor's Guide* for using the *Read On! II* series with conversational English (English Second Language) learners.

For Read On! II

Introduction

In this series, you will be using the traditional approach of teaching sight words in the context of the sentences in which they occur. These sight words will be used as the basis for phonics review and pattern instruction. All will be used to involve writing as an integral part of each lesson. Provide as much help as needed for learners as they read the sentences with you. You will be using this reading/assisted-reading approach as you expand into actual learner-generated stories in the other portions of your lessons.

The *Read On! II* series can be used with small groups of three to five learners, with individual learners or in a peer situation. The principles and practices are the same for each. At some point in the assisted reading exercises, you may feel more comfortable reading with individual learners or with two or three, but that is not absolutely necessary. Do whatever is comfortable and satisfying for your learners and for you.

Directions

Specific directions for the instructor appear throughout each textbook opposite the learners' pages. The following are general directions designed to give an overview of the activities which will occur in any given lesson.

Preliminaries:

Give the **Placement Test** which accompanies the series in order to place the learners in the correct book and to learn which if any of the consonant letters will need to be taught using the *Tutor Resource Sheets.* These sheets are intended for use with learners at the beginning levels in the series.

The following materials will be needed for lessons: pen with dark ink, 3 x 5 cards (either cut in half or quarters), notebook for each learner.

Procedure:

(1) Prepare for your lesson by reading the passage aloud prior to meeting with your learners.

(2) Read the whole story to the learners and then return to the first selection to begin the chapter-by-chapter instruction. (The "Poison Puzzle" is an exception to this as you want to read all but the final chapter.)

Be sure to read in phrases and not word-by-word to your learners. This modeling will lead to fluency in your learners' reading. Fluency aids comprehension. Remember, reading is getting meaning from the page—if the sentences haven't been understood, then they haven't been read. Without comprehension, boredom sets in and independent reading will not take place.

(3) In the **Setting The Context** portion of the reading selection, discuss the passage. There will be suggestions given in the Tutor's Directions on each left-hand page. This context setting is important because it allows the reader (you or your learners) to bring to mind the knowledge and expectations about the situation being portrayed and thus will aid in reading. Have the student handle the book, looking through it for illustrations and familiar words. See *Instructor's Guide* for comprehension development ideas.

(4) After discussion, read the chapter to your learners having them follow along silently. Tell your learners that you will read the chapter to them, and that the regular print words (point them out) will be the ones which they will either learn during that lesson or have already learned in previous lessons.

(5) After reading the chapter, teach the lesson's words in a modified language experience approach (modified because the words to be learned directly are set by the design of the series rather than selected by the learner). Many words will be learned indirectly through peripheral learning as the passage and selected sentences are read again and again with the learners.

Sight words from the story will be taught in the context of the sentences in the story.

If the learner knows the target word already, make a word card of the word for use in activities, but do not go through the exercise of teaching the word.

a) You have already read the whole story to the learners. You have also (step 4 above) read them the chapter upon which the next lesson(s) will be based. At this point you will read the unit under study. (Towards the end of the book as the pace quickens, chapters will no longer be broken down into units.) Now, read the first unit again with you and the learners speaking at the same time. Your learners may be one beat behind you on the words of which they are not sure. This is called "echo reading" and this difference in rate is to be expected. Do not slow down. Read at a normal rate, running your finger along under the phrases, being careful not to read word-by-word. It might take a while to get accustomed to echo reading as we are not used to reading or talking in chorus.

b) Tell the learners which words you will be studying. (They are listed in the directions for each unit and on the learner's page.) Point to each target word as you say it. Have the learners repeat and point to each target word after you say it.

c) Read the sentences which contain the target words again. Have the learners read the sentences with you the second time through (echo reading).

[If working with a small group, have the entire group read the sentences. Then have each learner read the target words, beginning with the best reader in these early lessons. If working one-to-one for this portion of the lesson, have the learner read all the words being introduced in the unit. This general group-to-individual direction will hold for all the times the learners are asked to read the target words, a sentence, phrase or unit.]

d) Have each learner write each target word on a word card (one half or one quarter of a 3 x 5 card, cut ahead of time).

[If a learner has not written much, this will almost be a "drawing" exercise. Be patient and allow all the time needed. If the learners' handwriting is too large for the words to fit on each card, have the learners write the words on a full card or in their notebooks as you write the words on the smaller cards for their use. It is important to have each learner writing from the first lesson.]

e) Work with one word at a time. Have learners match each word with the word as it appears in the story. They should say the word as they match it.

f) Once all the sight words for that lesson have been read, written on cards, read again, and matched with the context, shuffle the word cards and have the learners read each one out of context, matching the card with the word in the story if needed. Use the word cards to build phrases. After several lessons, use the accumulated word cards to make more complex sentences and phrases.

g) Use the word cards in writing and game activites.

Word patterns also will be taught in the context of the story. Word cards will be made for each new word pattern learned.

[If you are unfamiliar with the concept of *word pattern* see *Read On! II Instructor's Guide* for a complete discussion and the "Scope and Sequence Chart" which lists those patterns taught in this series.]

a) Select a word containing the pattern you want to teach from among the sight words already taught.

b) Ask the learners to get their word card for the target pattern and read the word card to you.

c) The first few times you use pattern word technique, say "I'm going to show you a way to learn new words by changing just the first letter(s) of a word you already know. If this word is *sat* [Write as you say the word. Make sure that each learner can see what you are writing], what word is written if I change the *s* to *m*? [Write the second word under the first lining up the pattern as you ask the question.]

Once the idea of supplying the word in pattern or rhyme is established in the first few lessons, you can introduce pattern in the following way: As you write, say "If this word is *get,* what is this word _____?" Fill in the second word in the pattern and wait for a response; if none is given, supply it and go on to the third word in the pattern.

Example: "If this word is *make* what is this word? (fake), and this word? (rake)." Ask for other words in the pattern. You might say "We're going to make a list of all the words you know and will be able to read because you know now that the -am in 'am' has the same sound as -am in Sam, and jam and. . ." Read quickly through the list on the board or your paper to establish the rhythm and make it easier for the next word in the pattern to be thought of and suggested. c) After you have gotten other suggestions and discussed the meaning of any of the obscure ones say "Get your notebooks and write -am (or whatever the pattern is you're working with) at the top of the page.

"The - means that letters can be put in front of the -*am* to make a word." Let learners supply rhyming words; have them write them in their notebooks. Treat this learning and suggesting as a game. Ask each learner in turn to name a word in pattern and to put it in a sentence. At the end of the lesson, ask them to write a sentence for each word learned during the lesson.

d) Have learners make a word card for each pattern word suggested. This can be done at the end of the lesson or for home practice.

Phonics, the knowledge of consonant sound/symbol relationships, is checked during the lesson, but the actual teaching takes place at the end of the reading portion of the lesson and is based on the *Tutor Resource Sheets* which accompany the series.

a) Ask the learner to find a specific word card which they have already made for a sight or patterned word in the lesson which begins with the letter you want to check.

b) Ask the learner to read the word, and then to tell you the name of the letter that begins the word. Then ask for the sound of that letter. If it is known, say "Good" and go on. If it isn't known, tell the learner the name of the letter and its sound in that word, note that you will need to teach that letter at the end of the reading portion of the lesson and go on.

(6) After the direct instruction portion of the lesson **(sight words, pattern, phonics),** you will do **Assisted Reading** exercises which will give learners more practice in reading the words in context:

a) Read the passage to the learners again. This will put the pieces back together for them. Ask the learners to follow along as you read all the words, again reminding them to pay attention to words they will be able to read, that is, the words in regular type.

b) You and your learners (or an individual student) then read the passage aloud at the same time. This is echo reading as described above under "Sight Words."

c) In the next read-through, you read softly, stopping at the words in regular print to allow learners to fill in the word they should know. Read softly enough so that the learners can read any of the other words known to them. With practice, a natural assisted reading pattern will emerge.

(7) You will use writing exercises to give the learners a chance to place the words being learned into new contexts, demonstrating comprehension of the word being learned.

(8) Each learner should keep a notebook of his or her writing activities.

(9) Expansion exercises are suggested at the end of each lesson, and in the workbooks which accompany each text. These are designed to allow each lesson to be tailored to individual learner's goals.

Vital Information for the Instructor

Watch your learners for signs of fatigue or boredom. Adjust to the individual learner's pace. If teaching more than one learner in a small group you might adjust by having the more advanced learner review on his or her own, or give the slower learner extra help while the others in the small group work on other projects together. If there is a great difference in ability among learners in a group, you may want to give extra help to the slower learner prior to introducing that day's work to the group as a whole.

Any time you want to do the exercises as an individual activity rather than a group activity, call on individual learners or, in later lessons, have learners work in pairs while you give assistance as needed or asked. For additional direction in working with small groups see *Tutoring Small Groups: Basic Reading* (LVA, 1985).

Most chapters in the text are broken into two or three lessons. This is done to help you pace the instruction to individual capabilities. Some groups might stop after each lesson, others might do two or even three lessons on any given day. You will become familiar with the learners' capabilities and be able to adjust the instruction accordingly.

If a unit is not completed in one day's lesson, give the word cards just completed to the learners for them to work with in preparation for the next lesson just as if the whole lesson had been completed. Also, assign workbook activities as appropriate either for homework or for class practice. In the next lesson, repeat the unit.

Much valuable home practice can be provided to the learners if you tape record yourself reading the passages. Identify each passage on the tape by title and page number. Give these tapes to the learners to use as review by following along in their books as you read the passages on tape they have been studying.

At the end of each textbook, there are expansion exercises for further activities to be carried out which will allow you to tailor the set vocabulary to the particular interests of the learners as well as giving writing and word identification practice.

Tutor Directions Chapter One

IMPORTANT: Read "General Directions" in front of book and "Vital Information for the Tutor" before proceeding.

Notes for Unit One of *Let Me Tell You a Story:* You will be given extremely detailed instructions for guiding the lessons in this chapter. This first chapter with its words to be learned might cover several lessons. Subsequent chapters might take less time. Use your judgment as to how much your Learners are able to absorb during the direct teaching (Sight Words, Pattern, Phonics) of a session and what will have to be reinforced in the activities.

Do prompt and reread to the Learners during the lessons. Writing assignments, games using the word cards, language experience activities and the workbooks are additional ways of providing needed repetition and reinforcement. The units can be read again and again during sessions. This modeling is a very effective way of teaching both actual words and the idea of sound/symbol relationship. The units can also be suggested as home reading between lessons.

Recording the whole story (indicating chapter breaks) for the Learners to read along with will provide additional practice. This practice will both speed up learning of the target words and extend the peripheral learning of non-target words.

Recording the lesson unit by unit, listing the sight words to be written and practiced, as well as the pattern to be learned, will provide an opportunity for independent study or peer work in each lesson. This recording could also provide additional, independent study for the more beginning Learners in a small group or classroom situation. If you decide to make this kind of a recording, be sure to include pauses for Learner responses.

Have a world map at the lesson site. Point out the location of the folktales.

Unit 42

Setting the Context

Tutor/Learners—[Introduce/ask about/discuss the topic. Explain to Learners that these are stories within a story.] The old storyteller is speaking to the listeners in a poetic, musical way. Since the beginning of time, every country has had its storytellers. Why were they important? (Discuss: Many people had no written language; many people could not read.) [Have Learners read titles and look at illustrations. Discuss what the stories might be about. Give positive response.]

Vocabulary   peer, possibilities, incredible, continents, heart [poetic]

Tutors/Learners—[Read Introduction by sentences, phrases, finger sliding under words. Learners follow silently. Learners then read aloud with you (echo reading).]

Tutor—[Work with one vocabulary word at a time. Say the word as you write it.] Copy the word **peer** on a 3 x 5 card. Find **peer** in the story. Read the sentence with me. What do you think **peer** might mean? (Discuss) [Tell the Learners that, as a group, you will check the meaning they come up with against the dictionary meaning. Explain to Learners why we use a dictionary (to learn meanings of words and the spelling of words). Explain the structure of a dictionary.]
   Think of a dictionary as being in three parts. Words beginning with the letters A through F would be found in the first third of the dictionary; words beginning with G through O would be found in the middle third of the dictionary; and words beginning with the letters P through Z would be found in the last third of the dictionary. [It is helpful to have the alphabet from the *Tutor Resource Sheets* or workbooks available so that the Learners can check on the order of the letters.]
   Look for **peer** in the dictionary. Since **peer** begins with the letter p, find the P section in the dictionary. Now, look at the second letter in **peer.** What is it? (e) O.K., now look in the P section of the dictionary for words that begin with p-e. Then look for the next letter, continuing this process until you find the word. When you find **peer,** read the definitions (meanings) and decide which is the correct meaning as **peer** is used in the story. (Discuss) [Accept tentative definitions. Restate the definition in the group's own words. Follow this pattern for each of the vocabulary words.]
   Get your vocabulary card for **peer.** On the back of the card, write the definition (meaning) of the word. Write a sentence using the word **peer.**
   [Repeat this procedure for each of the vocabulary words.]

Sight Words /story, dark, glowing, peer, outward, meaning, throat, humor, always, stories, heart, believe, ourselves/

Tutor/Learners—[Re-read Unit 42, Learners follow silently. Then Learners read aloud with you (echo reading).]

Let Me Tell You a Story

Unit 42

The old teller of **tales** sat close to the fire. The **leaping flames traced shadows** upon her dark, **wrinkled** face. Children and their parents **huddled** close, their faces glowing with **anticipation**. The old woman's eyes seemed to peer far **beyond** the small **gathering**. They peered outward into a **sea** of stars and **possibilities**; they peered inward into the **deepest** meaning of words and **ideas**.

She cleared her throat and the **entire gathering** became **hushed**. When she spoke, she **held** everyone's **attention**. Her voice was clear and **warm**, filled with **wisdom** and humor. And always, there was her **incredible** smile **brightening** all that it **touched**.

"I have **traveled** far," she said slowly. "I have heard many **remarkable** stories told by **storytellers** around **campfires** on many **continents**. I have found that their heart and **wisdom** are our heart and **wisdom**. I believe we are all one people **seeking** the same thing: a **knowledge** of ourselves."

/story, dark, glowing, peer, outward, meaning, throat, humor, always, stories, heart, believe, ourselves/

Tutor—We'll study these words in this first unit. I'll read them first. [Point to each sight word as you say it.] **story, dark, glowing, peer, outward, meaning, throat, humor, always, stories, heart, believe, ourselves**

Tutor—Now, you pick out the words and each of you read one. [If a Learner hesitates a long time, say the word while pointing to it.]

Learners—story, dark, glowing, peer, outward, meaning, throat, humor, always, stories, heart, believe, ourselves

Tutor—Yes, **story, dark, glowing, peer, outward, meaning, throat, humor, always, stories, heart, believe, ourselves.** [Quickly read the unit again. Put the sentences back together with the right intonation.]

Tutor—Now copy the words we're learning from the story on these separate cards. [Use quartered 3 x 5 cards.] If you already know how to read the word, copy it anyway so you'll have the word card to use in other activities we'll be doing. (Learners copy the words.)

Tutor—Look at your word cards and read them to me. [Read any word Learners hesitate on.]

Learners—(Read)

Tutor—O.K. I'm going to mix up the cards, and you read them to me. If you don't know a word, match the word card with the word in the sentence, then read it. We'll go through the card collection three times.

Learners—(Read the words in order given by the tutor.)

Tutor—O.K. Now I'm going to build a group of words. You read them after me. [Assume vocabulary from previous lessons, use the new cards, writing in the other words, and build a word group such as: **I like stories with humor.** Read it and have the learners read it after you. Go over it again until it is read as a unit and not word-by-word or syllable-by-syllable. READ IN MEANINGFUL UNITS.]

Learners—(Read)

Pattern 1 /-ark/

Tutor—Get your word card for **dark** and read it. If this word is **dark**, what is this word? **(park)**

[As you speak, write the word **park** on a chalkboard, or on an easel pad that the Learners can see. Wait for Learner's response.]

Now, write **-ark** at the top of a page in your notebook. Under it write **dark**, lining up the **-ark** part of the words. [Read words quickly.] What other words that either rhyme with **dark** and **park** or contain the pattern **ark (remark)** can you add to our list? [Accept any other words in the pattern that they suggest. Discuss meaning.]

12

Your sight word cards might look like this

story	throat
dark	humor
glowing	always
peer	stories
outward	heart
meaning	believe

ourselves

Pattern 2 /-ean/

Tutor—[Have Learners find word card for **meaning** and read it aloud. If this word is **meaning**, what is this word? **(mean)**

[As you speak, write the word **mean** so the Learners can see it and wait for their response.] Now, what is this word? **(lean)**

[Continue to teach pattern as shown above.]

Pattern 3 /-ow/

Tutor—[Have Learners find the word card for **glowing** and read it aloud.] If this word is **glowing**, what is this word? **(glow)** And this word? **(row, grow, low)** [Continue teaching pattern as shown above.]

End of Chapter Assisted Reading

(1) Read chapter to Learners
(2) Read chapter with Learners [echo reading]
(3) Read chapter with Learners [shared reading]

End of Chapter Activities

[Have Learners (1) make word cards for words in pattern (listed on card in back of text); (2) do integrated workbook activities; (3) see additional "Suggested Activities" at end of text.]

Your word pattern page might look like this

-ean

mean

meaning

lean

clean

jean

Unit 43

Setting the Context

Tutor/Learners—[Introduce/ask about/discuss the topic. Have Learners read title, look at illustration. Explain that everyone has his or her own idea of what happens to us after we die.] Many people in India believe we come back to earth in a different form. Millions believe that our souls go to heaven or hell. Others are sure that when we die, that's the end of it. In this story we'll read about three men who believe that life goes on just as it did before they died. What do you believe happens when we die? [Tutor give positive response. It is important not to promote your personal beliefs but to accept the Learners' ideas. Find Nigeria on a world map. Read whole story by sentences, phrases, finger sliding under words. Learners follow silently.]

43A Vocabulary competition, stubborn, Africa, reputation, simple

Tutor/Learners—[Read Unit 43A, Learners follow silently; Learners then read aloud with you (echo reading). Continue to slide finger under words each time you read a selection.]

Tutor—[Work with one vocabulary word at a time; say the word as you write it.] Copy the word **competition** on a 3 x 5 card. Find this word in the title. What do you think it might mean? [Accept tentative definitions. If none is correct, refer Learners to dictionary. Suggest that Learners tell about competitions they have taken part in (games, contests, etc.). Restate the definition in the group's own words.]

Get your vocabulary card for **competition**. On the back of the card, write the definition (meaning) of the word. Write a sentence using the word **competition**.

[Repeat this procedure for each of the vocabulary words.]

Sight Words /both, Africa, river, debts, much, richest, fact, himself, collector/

Tutor/Learners—[Re-read Unit 43A, Learners follow silently; Learners then read aloud with you (echo reading). Then read sight words, pointing to each word as you say it. Learners copy words on word cards, saying each one as it is written.

Teach sight words as previously shown: review/mix the order of the cards/add word cards of previously learned words/make sentences with cards such as: **The richest men never pay their debts.**]

The Competition

Unit 43A

*"We have all **known vain** people and **stubborn** people. Both are, **indeed**, very trying **sorts**. In Africa, in a country called **Nigeria**, they tell a story about what happens when **vanity** and **stubborness** are **combined**."*

In a village near the **Benue** River in **Nigeria** there lived a man who never **repaid** his debts. No matter how much his neighbors **pleaded** with him or **tried** to shame him, he would not pay. It was not a matter of his being **unable** to repay his debts. He was one of the richest men in the village. No, he just **refused** to pay his debts. In fact, he was very **proud** of his **reputation** for never having **repaid** a debt.

One day, a **simple** but **curious** man was passing by just as a **large**, **stern** looking man was knocking on the door of this great debtor. When the **borrower** opened the door, the **large** man **introduced** himself as a bill collector. He **demanded** that the **borrower** repay a debt he owed to one of his neighbors.

/both, Africa, river, debts, much, richest, fact, himself, collector/

17

Pattern 1 /act/

Tutor—Get your word card for **actor**. If this word is **actor**, what is this word? **(act)** [Write the word as you say it.] And this word? **(fact)** And this word? **(factory)** Remember the sound of **y** at the end of a word. What other words rhyme with **act** or contain the **act** pattern? **(action, fraction)**

[Have Learners suggest new words. Discuss meanings and add to list. Have Learners write pattern and patterned words in their notebooks.]

Pattern 2 /-est/

Tutor—[Give an example to the Learners of the superlative such as: "I knew a **rich** man. Then I met a **richer** man. But the third man I met was the **richest** man of all."] We use **-est** on words to show the superlative form of the word. We say **happy**, then **happier**. What is the next word, the superlative?

Learners—happiest

Tutor—And **dark**?

Learners—dark, darker, darkest

Tutor—What other words do you know that can follow this pattern? **(big, fine)**

Pattern 3 /-self/

Tutor—[Have Learners find word card for **himself** and read it aloud. Ask Learners to read the sentences on the facing page. Explain how the word **himself** reflects back and emphasizes the word **he** in the sample sentence: **He** did it **himself**.

Point out that the singular form, **self**, changes to **selves** in the plural. Have Learners write sentences using all forms of **self, selves**.]

End of Unit Assisted Reading

Tutor—[Read the unit first, Learners following silently. Then read it together (echo reading). Read a third time; Learners read the words they know, you read the others (shared reading).]

NOTE: If end of lesson, go to the accompanying workbook for integrated activities or to the "Suggested Activities" at the end of textbook or do writing activities which reflect the individual Learner's interests and concerns.

Self

I did it myself.

We did it ourselves.

You did it yourself.

You did it yourselves.

He did it himself.

She did it herself.

They did it themselves.

It did it itself.

43B Vocabulary uphold, insist, persistent, afterlife

Tutor/Learners—[Read Unit 43B, Learners follow silently; Learners then read aloud with you (echo reading). Continue to slide finger under words each time you read a selection.]

Tutor—[Work with one vocabulary word at a time; say the word as you write it.] Copy the vocabulary word, **uphold**, on a 3 x 5 card. Find this word in the story. Read the sentence with me. What do you think **uphold** might mean? [Accept tentative definitions. If none is correct, refer Learners to dictionary. Discuss which definition is most appropriate to the context. Restate the definition in the group's own words.]

 Get your vocabulary card for **uphold**. On the back of the card, write the definition (meaning) of the word. Write a sentence using the word **uphold**.

 [Repeat this procedure for each of the vocabulary words.]

Sight Words /debtor, owe, also, collect, argument, followed, beside, argued, contest/

Tutor/Learners—[Re-read Unit 43B, Learners follow silently; Learners then read aloud with you (echo reading). Then read sight words, pointing to each word as you say it. Learners copy words on word cards, saying each one as it is written.

 Teach sight words as previously shown: review/mix the order of the cards/add word cards of previously learned words/make sentences with cards such as: **He argued with her about the contest. He's a debtor, also.**]

Pattern /-or/

Tutor—[Teach words that end in the **-or** pattern such as **debtor**.] Get your word card for **debtor** and read it aloud. A **debtor** is a person who owes a debt—either money or services—to someone else. The **-or** ending in this case means "**one who**". Can you think of any other words that follow this pattern? (**actor, director**) [Write the words as you speak.]

 [Have Learners suggest new words. Discuss meanings and add to list. Have Learners write pattern and patterned words in their notebook.]

End of Unit Assisted Reading

Tutor—[Read the unit first, Learners following silently. Then read it together (echo reading). Read a third time; Learners read the words they know, you read the others (shared reading).]

End of Story Assisted Reading

 (1) Read story to Learners; (2) Read story with Learners [echo reading]; (3) Read story with Learners [shared reading].

End of Story Activities

 [Have Learners (1) make word cards for words in pattern (listed on card in back of text); (2) do integrated workbook activities; (3) see additional "Suggested Activities" at end of text.]

"You must be kidding," said the debtor. "Don't you know who I am? I owe **everyone** in this village and have never **repaid** a debt. **I'm** not going to start now. After all, I have a **reputation** to **uphold**."

"Well," said the bill collector, **puffing** out his chest, "I have a **reputation** to **uphold** also. I have been collecting bills all over this country and I have never yet **failed** to collect a debt. I **insist** that you pay up."

An argument followed and the **curious passerby** sat down on a small hill beside the road to listen.

The two men argued hour after hour and into the next day. At last, the debtor in a **desperate attempt** to get away from the **persistent** bill collector took his own life.

The bill collector, not wanting to be **beaten** by the **stubborn** debtor, **decided** that if he could not collect the debt in life, he would follow the debtor into the **afterlife**. So he took his life also.

The **passerby** had **become** so **interested** in the argument that he **decided** that he must see how it **turned** out. So he, too, took his life.

How this great contest was **settled**, no living person knows. And **honestly** I am not **interested** enough to follow them into the **afterlife** to find out. Are you?

/debtor, owe, also, collect, argument, followed, beside, argued, contest/

Unit 44

Setting the Context

Tutor/Learners—[Introduce/ask about/discuss the topic. Learners read title, look at illustration. Show Learners map of the world.] This story takes place on the island of Haiti. [Tutor point out Haiti on the map.] An island is a piece of land that is entirely surrounded by water. Haiti is hundreds of miles from the United States. [Point out the U.S. on the map, indicating New York City. Discuss travels Learners have taken, especially trips to ocean beaches; ask if they have ever seen a turtle or a pigeon. Give positive response. Read whole story by sentences, phrases, finger sliding under words. Learners follow silently.]

Vocabulary coastline, beach, promptly

Tutor/Learners—[Read Unit 44, Learners follow silently; Learners then read aloud with you (echo reading). Continue to slide finger under words each time you read a selection.]

Tutor—[Work with one vocabulary word at a time; say the word as you write it.] Copy the vocabulary word, **coastline**, on a 3 x 5 card. Find this word in the story. Read the sentence with me. What do you think **coastline** might mean? [Accept tentative definitions. If none is correct, refer Learners to dictionary. Discuss which definition is most appropriate to the context. Restate the definition in the group's own words.]

   Get your vocabulary card for **coastline**. On the back of the card, write the definition of the word. Write a sentence using the word **coastline**.

   [Repeat this procedure for each of the vocabulary words.]

Sight Words /island, decided, leave, I'll, mouth, ocean, agreed, eagerly, beak, toward, sea, goodbye, noticed, vine, surely/

Tutor/Learners—[Re-read Unit 44, Learners follow silently; Learners then read aloud with you (echo reading). Then read sight words, pointing to each word as you say it. Learners copy words on word cards, saying each one as it is written.

   Teach sight words as previously shown: review/mix the order of the cards/add word cards of previously learned words/make sentences with cards such as: **I went to the sea. She said goodbye when she got ready to leave.**]

Turtle and Pigeon

Unit 44

*"Now, let me tell you a story from the beautiful island of **Haiti**,"* the woman said.

And they all listened.

There was a time, long **ago**, when all the **pigeons** decided to leave **Haiti** and go to New **York** City. **Turtle** wanted to go also but he had no wings.

One **pigeon** felt **sorry** for **Turtle** and **offered** to take him **along**. "I'll hold one end of a **vine** in my mouth and you hold on to the other end," said **Pigeon**. "You cannot let go, no matter what happens because if you do, you will fall into the ocean."

23

Pattern 1 /I'll, you'll/

Tutor—[Have Learners find word card for **I'll**.] **I'll** is a short way to say **I will**, and **you'll** is a short way to say **you will**. We use these short cuts all the time when we speak. How would you shorten **he will**?

[Wait for Learners response. Teach pattern of contractions shown below on a chalkboard or an easel pad that everyone can see.]

I will	I'll		we will	we'll
you will	you'll		you will	you'll
he will	he'll			
she will	she'll		they will	they'll
it will	it'll			

Pattern 2 /-eak/

Tutor—[Teach words in the **-eak** pattern as in **beak**.] Get your word card for **beak** and read it. If this word is **beak**, what is this word? (**speak**) And this word? (**creak**)

[As you speak, write the word. Have Learners suggest new words, discuss meanings, add to list. Have Learners write pattern and patterned words in their notebooks.]

Pattern 3 /-ine/

Tutor—[Have Learners find word card for **vine** and read it aloud. Teach pattern **-ine** as shown above. (**vine, wine, whine**)]

Pattern 4 /-ly/

Tutor—[Ask Learners to find the word card for **eagerly**. Explain that the **-ly** ending shows how, when, or where something happened. [Write the words below on a chalkboard, or an easel pad that the Learners can see. Point out that if a word ends with the letter **y**, we change the **y** to **i** when adding **ly**.]

eager	eagerly
clear	clearly
happy	happily
strong	strongly
sure	surely
sad	sadly

End of Story Assisted Reading

(1) Read story to Learners
(2) Read story with Learners [echo reading]
(3) Read story with Learners [shared reading]

End of Story Activities

[Have Learners (1) make word cards for words in pattern (listed on card in back of text); (2) do integrated workbook activities; (3) see additional "Suggested Activities" at end of text.]

Turtle agreed eagerly and **grabbed** the end of the **vine** in his mouth. **Pigeon scooped** up the other end in his beak and flew into the air with **Turtle trailing** behind, his mouth **clamped** tightly to the **vine.** Off they flew toward the sea.

Just as they were passing over the **coastline** of the island, **Turtle** saw a **group** of animals **gathered** on the **beach.** They were **waving** and **shouting** goodbye to all the **birds flying** to New **York.** Soon they noticed **Pigeon carrying Turtle** at the end of the vine. The **crowd** stopped **waving** and began talking to each other.

"Surely that cannot be **Turtle** going to New **York** with the **birds,**" said one animal.

"But it is!" **replied** another.

Soon all the animals were **shouting** to **Turtle:** "**Turtle,** you are going to New **York** also! Even **Turtle** is going all the way to New **York!**"

Turtle was so **excited** and **proud** to hear **everyone** talking about him and **cheering** for him that he could not **resist** calling back to the **crowd**:

"Goodbye, goodbye!"

Having opened his mouth to speak these words, **Turtle promptly** fell into the sea.

And this, my friends is why today there are many **pigeons** in New **York** City but to find **turtles** by the hundreds you must go to **Haiti.**

/island, decided, leave, I'll, mouth, ocean, agreed, eagerly, beak, toward, sea, goodbye, noticed, vine, surely/

Unit 45

Setting the Context

Tutor/Learners—[Introduce/ask about/discuss the topic. Learners read title, look at illustration.] The title of this story is **"Justice,"** which means fair play. We'll read about a group of people who thought only of themselves and what was good for them. We call this being **self-centered**. (Discuss) [Give positive response. Read whole story by sentences, phrases, finger sliding under words. Learners follow silently.]

45A Vocabulary murdered, determined, verdict, cried out, reconsider, however

Tutor/Learners—[Read Unit 45A, Learners follow silently; Learners then read aloud with you (echo reading). Continue to slide finger along under words each time you read a selection.]

Tutor—[Work with one vocabulary word at a time; say the word as you write it.] Copy the vocabulary word, **murdered**, on a 3 x 5 card. Find this word in the story. Read the sentence with me. What do you think **murdered** might mean? [Accept tentative definitions. If none is correct, refer Learners to dictionary. Discuss which definition is most appropriate to the context. Restate the definition in the group's own words.]

Get your vocabulary card for **murdered**. On the back of the card, write the definition (meaning) of the word. Write a sentence using the word **murdered**.

[Repeat this procedure for each of the vocabulary words.]

Sight Words /justice, young, adults, judge, lived, murdered, brought, crime, verdict, shall, repair, cried/

Tutor/Learners—[Re-read Unit 45A, Learners follow silently; Learners then read aloud with you (echo reading). Then read sight words, pointing to each word as you say it. Learners copy words on word cards, saying each one as it is written.

Teach sight words as previously shown: review/mix the order of the cards/add word cards of previously learned words/make sentences with cards such as: **The judge asked the man what crime he had done.**]

Pattern 1 /-ive/

Tutor—[Have Learners find word card for **live** and read it aloud.] If this word is **live**, what is this word? (**give**)

[As you speak, write the word so that Learners can see. Wait for Learners response. Point out to Learners that **live** sounds the same as **give** and is not the same as the word **live** in **alive**.

Have Learners suggest new words. Discuss meanings, add to list. Have Learners write pattern and patterned words in their notebooks.]

26

Justice

Unit 45A

The old woman looked around the fire. Her **audience** sat **expectantly** before the fire waiting for another story. She smiled at the wide-eyed young ones and **stared wisely** at the adults.

She said, "In **Israel** I was told a story about a judge who lives in a town of very **foolish** people. It is said that this judge was a very **wise** man, but you may decide for yourselves."

One day in a small town, there was a great **tragedy**. The **shoemaker** had murdered one of his **customers**. He was brought before the town judge who **determined** that for his **terrible** crime the **shoemaker** should be **hanged**.

Pattern 2 /ry—ried/

Tutor—[Have Learners find word card for **cried** and read it aloud. Explain that **cried** is the past tense of **cry**. Ask Learners for other words that rhyme with **cry** (**fry, try**), listing both the present and past tense of each word in two columns. Continue teaching pattern as shown above.]

End of Unit Assisted Reading

Tutor—[Read the unit first, Learners following silently. Then read it together (echo reading). Read a third time; Learners read the words they know, you read the others (shared reading).]

Note: If end of lesson, go to the accompanying workbook for integrated activities or to the "Suggested Activities" at the end of the textbook or do writing activities which reflect the individual Learner's interest and concerns.

The townspeople were upset at the verdict. A man from the town **stood** up and **shouted**, "But, your **Honor**, this man is the only **shoemaker** in town. What shall we do if he is **hanged**? Who will make and repair our **shoes**?"

All the people of the town cried out as one, "Who, **indeed**, will mend our **shoes** and make our **boots**?"

/justice, young, adults, judge, lived, murdered, brought, crime, verdict, shall, repair, cried/

Unit 45B Vocabulary reconsider, however

Tutor/Learner—[Read Unit 45B, Learners follow silently; Learners then read aloud with you. Continue to slide finger under words each time you read a selection.]

Tutor—[Teach vocabulary words as shown in Unit 45A.]

Sight Words /self-centered, thought, reconsider, however, those/

Tutor/Learners—[Re-read Unit 45B, Learners follow silently; Learners then read aloud with you (echo reading). Then read sight words, pointing to each word as you say it. Learners copy words on word cards, saying each one as it is written.
    Continue teaching sight words as previously shown.]

Pattern /-ought/

Tutor—[Teach words in the **-ought** pattern as in **brought**.] Get your word card for **brought** and read it. If this word is **brought**, what is this word? **(thought)**
    [As you speak, write the word. Wait for Learner's response. Have Learners suggest new words, discuss meanings, add to list. Have Learners write pattern and patterned words in their notebooks.]

End of Unit Assisted Reading

Tutor—[Read the unit first, Learners following silently. Then read it together (echo reading). Read a third time; Learners read the words they know, you read the others (shared reading).]

End of Story Assisted Reading

    (1) Read story to Learners
    (2) Read story with Learners [echo reading]
    (3) Read story with Learners [shared reading]

End of Story Activities

    [Have Learners (1) make word cards for words in pattern (listed on card in back of text); (2) do integrated workbook activities; (3) see additional "Suggested Activities" at end of text.]

The judge was **dumbstruck** to hear the people **respond** in such a self-centered way. He thought for a **moment**, then he **nodded** his head and said, "Good townspeople, your **reasoning** has made me reconsider my verdict."

The townspeople were **relieved**. They were **hopeful** as they waited for the judge to give his new verdict.

"My good people," said the judge, "that which you have said is **true**. We have only one **shoemaker** so it would be very bad for the **community** to put him to death. However, since there are two **tailors** in the town, let one of them be **hanged instead**."

"Those people are just like some people we know here! one woman said and laughed.

"Yes, sometimes people are very self-centered. Maybe it's good to have stories to make us think," said a man.

/self-centered, thought, reconsider, however, those/

Unit 46

Setting the Context

Tutor/Learners—[Introduce/ask about/discuss the topic. Have Learners read title, look at illustration.] All of us have played tricks on someone at one time or another, but we're going to read about Coyote who played tricks on people all the time. This story is from the southwest United States. [Point out the area on your map.] Have any of you been in the southwest? The northwest? [Point out northwest on the map.] (Discussion) [Give positive response. Read whole story by sentences, phrases, finger sliding under words. Learners follow silently.]

46A Vocabulary inventive, trickster, Native American, southwest, whether or not, exaggerated, medicine bag

Tutors/Learners—[Read Unit 46A, Learners follow silently; Learners then read aloud with you (echo reading). Continue to slide finger along under words each time you read a selection.]

Tutor—[Work with one vocabulary word at a time; say the word as you write it.] Copy the vocabulary word, **inventive**, on a 3 x 5 card. Find this word in the story. Read the sentence with me. What do you think **inventive** might mean? [Accept tentative definitions. If none is correct, refer Learners to dictionary. Discuss which definition is most appropriate to the context. Restate the definition in the group's own words.]

Get your vocabulary card for **inventive**. On the back of the card, write the definition of the word. Write a sentence using the word **inventive**.

[Repeat this procedure for each of the vocabulary words.]

Coyote and the **Cowboy**

Unit 46A

*"Yes," the old woman said, almost to herself. "Yes, we are such children, so **full** of ourselves and so eager for **simple** answers to **hard** questions. Yet, also like children, we are so **inventive**, so clever. Like **Coyote**, that **trickster** the **Native Americans** of the **southwest** United States tell us about. Such a **clever fellow**, that one. Not always so **nice**, but always **clever**.*

*"If you are **wondering** whether **Coyote** is a man or an animal, do not **worry**. The **Coyote** stories are set in a **long-ago** time when **humans** and animals **behaved** very much alike."*

Coyote was sitting on a **rock**, resting after a long day of walking down dusty roads. His feet **hurt**, his throat was dry and his eyes **stung** from the dust. In the **distance** he saw a **cloud** of dust **approaching**. Soon he could make out a man on **horseback**.

33

Sight Words /questions, United States, whether, dusty, I've, left, famous, you're, I'm, you've, really, dare, little, partner, medicine/

Tutor/Learners—[Re-read Unit 46A, Learners follow silently; Learners then read aloud with you (echo reading). Then read sight words, pointing to each word as you say it. Learners copy words on word cards, saying each one as it is written.

Teach sight words as previously shown: review/mix the order of the cards/add word cards of previously learned words/make sentences with cards such as: **My car is dusty. You're really famous in the United States.**]

A **cowboy rode** up and stopped beside **Coyote**. He looked down and said to **Coyote**, "Are you the **coyote** I've heard so much about? The one that plays all the tricks on people?"

"No," said **Coyote**, and looked off into the **distance**.

"Sure you are," said the **Cowboy**. "I've been following you for days, since you left the town back there. **Everybody** there said you were the famous **Coyote**, the great **trickster**. Now don't kid me. You're him, aren't you?"

"**Okay**, you're right. I'm the **coyote** you've heard about, but believe me, those stories you hear are **exaggerated**. I'm not really like that at all." **Coyote** slid down off the **rock** and began walking down the road.

The **cowboy** followed. "Come on, now. I know what's what. You're the great trickster **Coyote**. So come on, trick me. I dare you to try your old bag of tricks on me, Little Partner."

"**Okay**," **sighed Coyote**. "You're right about me, but I cannot trick you today because I am very **tired** and my trickster medicine bag is way back west. It would take me days to walk there."

/questions, United States, whether, dusty, I've, left, famous, you're, I'm, you've, really, dare, little, partner, medicine/

Pattern 1 /have—has/

Tutor—[Teach the **have/has** contraction by explaining that they are short cuts for **I have, he has,** etc.] We use these short cuts often when we talk. When we write them, we use an apostrophe to show that some letters have been left out. Look at List A on the next page, follow as I read it. [Read across.] Now you read List A.

Pattern 2 /to be/

Tutor—[Teach **to be** contractions as shown above using List B.] Notice that **he's, she's** and **it's** could mean either **he has, she has, it has** or **he is, she is, it is.** You can only tell if **he's** is **he has** or **he is** from the meaning of the sentence it is in: **He's come** means **He has come; He's good** means **He is good**.

End of Unit Assisted Reading

Tutor—[Read the unit first, Learners following silently. Then read it together (echo reading). Read a third time; Learners read the words they know, you read the others (shared reading).]

NOTE: If end of the lesson, go to the accompanying workbook for integrated activities or to the "Suggested Activities" at the end of textbook or do writing activities which reflect the individual Learner's interests and concerns.

Contractions

List A

I have	I've	we have	we've
you have	you've	you have	you've
he has	he's		
she has	she's	they have	they've
it has	it's		

List B

I am	I'm	we are	we're
you are	you're	you are	you're
he is	he's		
she is	she's	they are	they're
it is	it's		

46B Vocabulary good fortune, scooped, cactus

Tutor/Learners—[Read Unit 46B, Learners follow silently; Learners then read aloud with you (echo reading). Continue to slide finger under words each time you read a selection.]

Tutor—[Teach vocabulary words as shown in preceding unit.]

Sight Words /chance, trickster, idea, borrow, horse, easily, hardly, fortune, opposite, mount, again/

Tutor/Learners—[Re-read Unit 46B, Learners follow silently; Learners then read aloud with you (echo reading). Then read sight words, pointing to each word as you say it. Learners copy onto word cards, saying each word as it is written.
   Teach sight words as previously shown.]

Pattern 1 /-ount/

Tutor—[Teach words in the **-ount** pattern.] Get your word card for **mount** and read it. If this word is **mount**, what is this word? (**count**) [Write the word as you say it. Wait for Learners' response.] Can you think of other rhyming words or words like **mountain** that contain the pattern **-ount** but don't rhyme? (**county**)
   [Have Learners suggest new words, discuss meanings, add to list. Have Learners write the pattern and pattern words in their notebooks.]

Pattern 2 /-orrow/

Tutor—[Teach words in the **-orrow** pattern. Have Learners find word card for **borrow** and read it aloud. Teach pattern as shown above. (**sorrow, tomorrow**)]

Pattern 3 /-er/

Tutor—[Teach words that end in the **-er** pattern using the word card for borrow.] If this word is **borrow**, what is this word? (**borrower**) [Explain to Learners that the **-er** ending, like the **-or** ending in Unit 43B, means "**one who**" ("one who" borrows). Offer some examples. (**buyer, seller, learner**) Continue teaching pattern as shown above.]

Pattern 4 /-ster/

Tutor—[Teach words in the **-ster** pattern. Point out that the endings **-ster, -er** and **-or** can all mean "**one who**."
   Teach pattern as previously shown. (**gangster, teamster**)]

End of Unit Assisted Reading

Tutor—[Read the unit first, Learners following silently. Then read it together (echo reading). Read a third time; Learners read the words they know, you read the others (shared reading).]

The **cowboy** was **disappointed** at not having a chance to show the great trickster, **Coyote**, that he could not be tricked by him. All of a sudden his face lit up as he said, "Listen, **Coyote**. I have an idea. Why don't you borrow my horse and go get your medicine bag. Riding will take much less time than walking and then you can try your **cleverness** out on me. You'll see then that I'm no **fool** like all the others you take **advantage** of so easily."

Coyote could hardly believe his good fortune at having met up with such a **numbskull**.

"Well, **okay**," said **Coyote** as the **cowboy climbed** down from his horse. As **Coyote** went around to the opposite side of the horse from the **cowboy**, he scooped up a small cactus. He took the horse's **reins** in one hand, and as he tried to mount the horse, he **jabbed** it with the **cactus**. The horse reared and would not let **Coyote** mount.

"**Ah**, you see," said **Coyote**. "He knows I am not you and he will not let me mount. I have an idea. Give me your hat. That way he will think I am you and will let me ride him."

This seemed like a very **clever** idea to the **cowboy** so he took off his hat and gave it to **Coyote**.

Coyote once again tried to mount the horse, giving him another **jab** with the **cactus**. The horse **once** again **refused** to let him mount.

/chance, trickster, idea, borrow, horse, easily, hardly, fortune, opposite, mount, again/

39

46C Vocabulary disguise, perhaps, resist, the logic

Tutor/Learners—[Read Unit 46C, Learners follow silently; Learners then read aloud with you (echo reading). Continue to slide finger under words each time you read a selection.

Tutor—[Teach vocabulary words as previously shown.]

Sight Words /perhaps, disguise, jacket, allow, secretly, jabbing, shiny, boots, belt, sadly, pants, short, nice/

Tutor/Learners—[Re-read Unit 46C, Learners follow silently; Learners then read aloud with you (echo reading). Then read sight words, pointing to each word as you say it. Learners copy words on word cards, saying each one as it is written.
   Teach sight words as previously shown: review/mix the order of the cards/add word cards of previously learned words/make sentences with cards such as: **I wore my brother's jacket and pants as a disguise. I have shiny new boots.**]

Pattern 1 /-elt/

Tutor—[Teach words in the **-elt** pattern as in **belt.**] Get your word card for **belt** and read it. If this word is **belt**, what is this word? (**melt, felt**)
   [As you speak, write the word. Wait for Learner's response. Have Learners suggest new words, discuss meanings, add to list. Have Learners write pattern and patterned words in their notebooks.]

Pattern 2 /-ice/

Tutor—[Have Learners get word card for **nice** and read it aloud. Teach **-ice** pattern as shown above. (**rice, price**)]

"I see," said **Coyote**, "that my **disguise** is not good enough to **fool** this **splendid** animal of yours. Perhaps if you gave me your jacket I would look more like you and he will allow me to get on."

The **cowboy** took off his jacket and **tossed** it to **Coyote**, to trick the horse into giving **Coyote** a ride.

When **Coyote** tried to get on while secretly jabbing the **poor** horse with the **cactus**, the horse again **jumped** away.

"Wait," said the **cowboy**. "He is used to seeing my shiny guns and hearing my **jingling spurs**." The **cowboy** sat down in the road, pulled off his boots and **spurs** and gave them to **Coyote**. Standing, he **unbuckled** his gun belt and gave it, too, to **Coyote**.

Pattern 3 /-y/

Tutor—[Make a list of these words: **dust, shine, leak** and **show**. Read the list to the Learners. Ask them to rewrite the words adding the **-y** ending. Point out that in words that end in **e**, you drop the **e** before adding the **y**.]

End of Unit Assisted Reading

Tutor—[Read the unit first, Learners following silently. Then read it together (echo reading). Read a third time; Learners read the words they know, you read the others (shared reading).]

End of Story Assisted Reading

(1) Read story to Learners
(2) Read story with Learners [echo reading]
(3) Read story with Learners [shared reading]

End of Story Activities

[Have Learners (1) make word cards for words in pattern (listed on card in back of text); (2) do integrated workbook activities; (3) see additional "Suggested Activities" at end of text.]

After putting on boots, **spurs** and guns, **Coyote once** again tried to mount the horse. Again, he secretly poked the animal with the small **cactus** and the horse **jumped** away, **refusing** to let him ride.

Coyote looked sadly at the **cowboy**. "The only thing left is for you to give me your pants. Then, he cannot help but **mistake** me for you."

The **cowboy**, unable to **resist** the **logic** of this argument, took off his pants and handed them over. **Coyote immediately** put them on, hopped upon the horse and **rode** away. When he had **ridden** a short **distance**, **Coyote** stopped and **turned** back toward the cowboy. "Say, **cowboy**, now you know it for sure. I am the **cleverest Coyote** in these parts. Have a nice walk, Little Partner!"

/perhaps, disguise, jacket, allow, secretly, jabbing, shiny, boots, belt, sadly, pants, short, nice/

Unit 47

Setting the Context

Tutor/Learners—[Introduce/ask about/discuss the topic. Have Learners read title, look at illustration.] We all dream and for most of us, our dreams have meanings that are sometimes hard for us to understand. The *Bible* speaks often of dreams. Joseph told the ruler of Egypt what his dreams meant and saved Egypt from a famine. Sometimes we dream the same dream over and over. We read of people having visions, which are like dreams except they happen when the person is awake. We all are fascinated by stories about ghosts, and many people believe in them. There is a ghost in this story, but not the Halloween scary kind! (Discuss) [Give positive response. Read whole story by sentences, phrases, finger sliding under words. Learners follow silently.]

47A Vocabulary curious world, Ireland, amazing, furnishings, experience, travels, "marvelous little house", presently

Tutors/Learners—[Read Unit 47A, Learners follow silently; Learners then read aloud with you (echo reading). Continue sliding finger under words each time you read a selection.]

Tutor—[Work with one vocabulary word at a time; say the word as you write it.] Copy the vocabulary word, **amazing**, on a 3 x 5 card. Find **amazing** in the story and read the sentence with me. What do you think **amazing** might mean? [Accept tentative definitions. If none is correct, refer Learners to dictionary. Discuss which definition is most appropriate to the context. Restate the definition in the group's own words. Explain the meaning of the quotation marks around "marvelous little house" as a quotation of the woman. The quotation marks around "travels" in the text indicate a humorous reference to her visits in her dreams.]

Get your vocabulary card for **amazing**. On the back of the card, write the definition of the word. Write a sentence using the word **amazing**.

[Repeat this procedure for each of the vocabulary words.]

Sight Words /house, dreams, strange, ghost, breakfast, husband, ever, warm, garden, exist, afterwards, family, forward/

Tutor/Learners—[Re-read Unit 47A; Learners follow silently; Learners then read aloud with you (echo reading). Then read sight words, pointing to each word as you say it. Learners copy words on word cards, saying each one as it is written.

Teach sight words as previously shown: review/mix the order of the cards/add word cards of previously learned words/make sentences with cards such as: **My husband works in the garden before breakfast. I dream of ghosts at Halloween.**]

The House of Dreams

Unit 47A

*The old woman sat very still while the **laughter** slowly died down. Then she began **drawing** strange **figures** at the **edge** of the **dying** fire. As she **silently stirred** the **ashes**, a stillness came over the **group**. They waited for her to speak.*

*Finally, she looked up at the **gathering**. "Strange things happen in this **curious** world of ours, things that we cannot understand. Ghost stories are told all over the world. I heard this story in **Ireland**."*

In **Ireland** there lived a woman who one day at breakfast told her husband and children about a dream she had had the night before. "It was a most **amazing** dream," she said. "I spent hours in one of the **loveliest** houses I have ever seen, or even **imagined**, for that matter. It was so warm, so **comfortable**. I felt that I really **belonged** there."

Pattern 1 /-ange/

Tutor—[Teach words in the **-ange** pattern as in **strange**.] Get your word card for **strange** and read it. If this word is **strange**, what is this word? **(arrange)**

[As you speak, write the word. Wait for Learner's response. Have Learners suggest new words, discuss meanings, add to list. Have Learners write pattern and patterned words in their notebooks.]

Pattern 2 /forward—backward/

Tutor—[Have Learners find word cards for all of the words they've learned so far that contain the pattern **-ward** and read them aloud. Teach pattern of **forward, backward, upward, downward** as indicating direction. Continue teaching pattern as shown above.]

End of Unit Assisted Reading

Tutor—[Read the unit first, Learners following silently. Then read it together (echo reading). Read a third time; Learners read the words they know, you read the others (shared reading).]

NOTE: If end of the lesson, go to the accompanying workbook for integrated activities or to the "Suggested Activities" at the end of textbook or do writing activities which reflect the individual Learner's interest and concerns.

She went on to **describe** in great **detail** the many rooms of the house, its garden and **lawns**, and all the **furnishings**. "I don't think that such a place could **possibly** exist outside of **heaven**!" she ended up.

The following day she **reported** that she had again spent the night **wandering** through her "dream house". And each morning for weeks afterwards she told of her **experiences** in the house of her nightly dreams.

Soon her "**travels**" became somewhat of a family joke. Around the breakfast table everyone would ask about her **latest visit** to her house. She would eagerly **describe** it, not noticing or not caring about the **sly glances** and quick **winks** her family **exchanged** when they thought she was not looking. She talked of how much she looked forward to going to bed at night, just so that she could spend time in her "**marvelous little house**". **Presently**, however, the **subject** of the house **faded** from **conversation**.

/house, dreams, strange, ghost, breakfast, husband, ever, warm, garden, exist, afterwards, family, forward/

47B Vocabulary England, London, beside herself, exclaimed, property

Tutor/Learners—[Read Unit 47B, Learners follow silently; Learners then read aloud with you (echo reading). Continue to slide finger under words each time you read a selection.]

Tutor—[Teach vocabulary words as previously shown. Make a special point of explaining the phrase **beside herself.**]

Sight Words /real estate, quite, front, shown, stranger, property, quickly, couple, sign, entering, bother, none/

Tutor/Learners—[Re-Read Unit 47B. Teach sight words as previously shown. Point out to Learners that the sound of **qu** is pronounced like **kw.**]

Pattern 1 /-eal/

Tutor—[Teach pattern **-eal** as in **real** as previously shown. (**seal, steal**) Teach **real estate** as a phrase because of its usefulness.]

Pattern 2 /-own/

Tutor—[Teach pattern **-own** as in **shown** as previously done. (**known, grown**)]

Years passed and the family **moved** to **England**. **Upon arriving** in **London**, they got in **touch** with many real estate **agents** to find a **comfortable** place to live. After many days of looking, they were taken to a place outside of **London**. As they neared the road **leading** to the house, the woman became quite **excited**. "That road looks very much like the one **leading** to the house in my dreams."

By the time they pulled up in front of the **building**, she was beside herself with **excitement**.

"This is it!" she cried. "This is my house!"

They were taken inside but before they could be shown around, the woman **exclaimed**, "No, wait! Let me tell you about the house." And she **described** in great **detail** all the rooms in the house as well as the garden out back.

The real estate **agent** was **amazed** that this stranger knew so much about the property. But when the family quickly said they wanted to buy the house, he didn't ask any questions. On their part, the couple found the price of the house very **reasonable**. All that they had to do next was to sign some **papers** at the real estate **office**.

End of Unit Assisted Reading

Tutor—[Read the unit first, Learners following silently. Then read it together (echo reading). Read a third time; Learners read the words they know, you read the others (shared reading).]

End of Story Assisted Reading

(1) Read story to Learners
(2) Read story with Learners [echo reading]
(3) Read story with Learners [shared reading]

End of Story Activities

[Have Learners (1) make word cards for words in pattern (listed on card in back of text); (2) do integrated workbook activities; (3) see additional "Suggested Activities" at end of text.]

Upon entering the real estate **office**, the woman noticed that the manager seemed **startled** when he saw her. She could not **imagine** why since she had never met him before. After all the **papers** had been signed, the husband asked the manager "Why was the house so **reasonably** priced? Surely the owner could have asked more for such a lovely house? Is there some **problem** with it?"

"Well," **replied** the manager, speaking **directly** to the woman, "now that you have already signed, I'll tell you. There have been **reports** that the house is **haunted** by a **mysterious** woman who **appears** nightly. But I really don't think it will be of much bother to you. You see, **madam**, I myself have seen the ghost and she is none other than yourself!"

/real estate, quite, front, shown, stranger, property, quickly, couple, sign, entering, bother, none/

Unit 48

Setting the Context

Tutor/Learners—[Introduce/ask about/discuss the topic/read previous unit. Have Learners read title, look at illustration. Point out China on the world map.] There were many men in old China who spent much time thinking about the meaning of life. They lived close to nature and knew many of nature's secrets. (Discuss) [Give positive response. Read whole story by sentences, phrases, finger sliding under words. Learners follow silently.]

48A Vocabulary scholars, torment, furthermore

Tutor/Learners—[Read Unit 48A, Learners follow silently; Learners then read aloud with you (echo reading). Continue to slide finger under words each time you read a selection.]

Tutor—[Work with one vocabulary word at a time; say the word as you write it.] Copy the word **scholars** on a 3 x 5 card. Find the word in the story and read the sentence with me. What do you think **scholar** might mean? [Accept tentative definitions. If none is correct, refer Learners to dictionary. Discuss which definition is most appropriate to the context. Restate the definition in the group's own words.]

Get your vocabulary card for **scholars**. On the back of the card, write the definition of the word. Write a sentence using **scholars**.

[Repeat this procedure for each of the vocabulary words.]

Sight Words /boy, carefully, careful, says, farmers, head, held, nose, soups, together, rang/

Tutor/Learners—[Re-read Unit 48A, Learners follow silently; Learners then read aloud with you (echo reading). Then read sight words, pointing to each word as you say it. Learners copy words on word cards, saying each one as it is written.

Teach sight words as previously shown: review/mix the order of the cards/add word cards of previously learned words/make sentences with cards such as: **The boy rang the bells carefully. I held my nose because of the skunk's smell.**]

Pattern 1 /-oy/

Tutor—[Teach words in the **-oy** pattern as in **boy**.] Get your word card for **boy** and read it. If this word is **boy**, what is this word? **(toy)**

[As you speak, write the word. Wait for Learner's response. Have Learners suggest new words, discuss meanings, add to list. Have Learners write pattern and patterned words in their notebooks.]

Pattern 2 /-ang/

Tutor—[Have Learners find word card for **rang** and read it aloud. Teach pattern **-ang** as shown above. **(sang, bang)**]

Hell and Heaven

*The old storyteller smiled and poked at the fire with a long, **slender** stick. Sparks **leaped** up and **scattered** into the darkness **above** the **flares.***

Wu Lei lived in **China.** He was a man of peace and like many men of peace, he was very **wise** and kind. People would come from **miles** around to **seek** his advice and to listen to his **views** on life and nature. In fact, he had on occasions been **visited** by **scholars** from as far away as **Russia** and **Japan.**

One day a young boy came to **Wu Lei's** home and found the **wise** man **busy removing weeds** from his garden. The boy **watched** the **elderly** man carefully pull out each **weed** by its **root** and place it in a basket at his **feet.**

"Why are you so careful?" asked the boy. "They are only **weeds.** My father **hates** them. He just **yanks** them out and throws them far away. He says they exist only to **torment** farmers."

Wu Lei turned to the boy and said, "That is what I used to think until the day I **stumbled** and fell head **first** into a **clump** of these **weeds.** Here, smell them." He held the small **basket** under the boy's nose.

"**Ahhh!**" said the boy in surprise. "They have such a strange, **delicious** smell. What are they?"

53

Pattern 3 /-ful/

Tutor—[Have Learners find word card for **careful** and read it aloud. Teach pattern **-ful** as shown above. (**hopeful, carefully**)]

End of Unit Assisted Reading

Tutor—[Read the unit first, Learners following silently. Then read it together (echo reading). Read a third time; Learners read the words they know, you read the others (shared reading).]

NOTE: If end of the lesson, go to the accompanying workbook for integrated activities or to the "Suggested Activities" at the end of textbook or do writing activities which reflect the individual Learner's interests and concerns.

"I do not know, but I have found that they give a **delicious flavor** to soups and cooked vegetables. **Furthermore,** they fill my house with a lovely **fragrance.** These **weeds** and I have learned to live together quite nicely." **Wu Lei's** laughter rang in his throat like so many **tiny brass** bells.

However, he noticed that the boy was not laughing with him.

/boy, carefully, careful, says, farmers, head, held, nose, soups, together, rang/

48B Vocabulary disturbed, eternal, meditation

Tutors/Learners—[Read Unit 48B, Learners follow silently; Learners then read aloud with you (echo reading). Continue to slide finger under words each time you read a selection.]

Tutor—[Teach vocabulary words as shown in preceding unit.]

Sight Words /troubling, son, troubled, become, learned, Heaven, burn, true, robe/

Tutor—[Re-read Unit 48B, Learners follow silently; Learners then read aloud with you (echo reading). Then read sight words, pointing to each word as you say it.
   Write **trouble** so the Learners can see. Under **trouble** write **troubled**, pointing out the **-ed** ending. Then under that, write **troubling**. Remind Learners that they drop the final **e** when adding these endings. Teach **learn, learned,** and **learning** in the same way. Continuing teaching sight words as previously shown.]

Pattern /-urn/

Tutor—[Teach words in the **-urn** pattern.] If this word is **burn** what is this word? (**turn**)
   [Write the word as you say it. Wait for Learners response. Have Learners suggest new words, discuss meanings, add to list. Have Learners write the pattern and pattern words in their notebooks.]

End of Unit Assisted Reading

Tutor—[Read the unit first, Learners following silently. Then read it together (echo reading). Read a third time; Learners read the words they know, you read the others (shared reading).]

NOTE: If end of the lesson, go to the accompanying workbook for integrated activities or to the "Suggested Activities" at the end of textbook or do writing activities which reflect the individual Learner's interests and concerns.

"What is troubling you, my son?" he asked.

"**Sir,**" said the boy, "I am very troubled." The young boy told **Wu Lei** how **disturbed** he had become after learning about Hell. He had learned that Hell was a **terrible** place where people burned in **eternal** flames. He had been told that Hell was where **sinners** went and that all people were **sinners.**

Wu Lei was very unhappy when he heard this. "Didn't you hear about Heaven, also?" he asked.

"**Oh, yes,**" said the boy, "but you have to be so **terribly** good to go there. I don't think I can be that good. And I don't want to burn in Hell. Please, tell me, is it true what they say about Heaven and Hell?"

Wu Lei thought for a **moment** then took the boy into his house. He took a beautiful dark robe from his **closet** and handed it to the boy. "These things are too important for us to **accept blindly** what others may say. We must find our own answers to questions like these. Here, take my **meditation** robe and sit in the garden until you have found your answer."

/troubling, son, troubled, become, learned, Heaven, burn, true, robe/

48C Vocabulary transported, despite, thereafter

Tutors/Learners—[Read Unit 48C, Learners follow silently; Learners then read aloud with you (echo reading). Continuing to slide finger under words each time you read a selection.]

Tutor—[Teach vocabulary words as shown in Unit 48A.]

Sight Words /huge, sorts, food, though, yard, feed, large, morning, gently, yes, weeding, weeded, Sunday/

Tutor—[Re-read Unit 48C, Learners follow silently; Learners then read aloud with you (echo reading). Tutor then read and point to each sight word.
   Teach Sight Words as previously shown.]

Pattern 1 /-eed/

Tutor—[Teach words in the **-eed** pattern.] Get your word card for **weed**. If this word is **weed** what is this word? (**seed**)
   [Write the word as you say it. Wait for Learners response. Have Learners suggest new words, discuss meanings, add to list. Have Learners write the pattern and pattern words in their notebooks.]

Pattern 2 /-ard/

Tutor—[Have Learners find word card for **yard** and read it aloud. Teach pattern **-ard** as shown above. (**hard, card**)]

The boy sat in the garden **meditating** for many hours. In the middle of the night, he suddenly found himself **transported** to Hell. There he saw many people sitting around a huge table **covered** with all sorts of **wonderful** food. But there was something strange about the place. Even though there was **plenty** to eat, all the people were **thin** and **starving.**

The boy could not understand this until he noticed that all the people had to eat with were yard-long **chopsticks.** The **chopsticks** were so long that the people could not feed themselves and so they were all **wasting** away.

"So this is Hell," thought the boy. "How **cruel** the **Creator** must be only to give them yard-long **chopsticks.**"

Suddenly, the boy felt as if a great **wind** had picked him up and **carried** him away. Before he knew it he was in Heaven.

He was very surprised to find another large room with many people sitting around a **huge** table. There was much **delicious** food here also. But these people were very happy and **well-fed despite** having only yard-long **chopsticks** with which to eat.

The boy smiled with understanding as he **watched** the people reaching across the table to feed each other with their long **chopsticks.**

End of Unit Assisted Reading

Tutor—[Read the unit first, Learners following silently. Then read it together (echo reading). Read a third time; Learners read the words they know, you read the others (shared reading).]

End of Story Assisted Reading

(1) Read story to Learners
(2) Read story with Learners [echo reading]
(3) Read story with Learners [shared reading]

End of Story Activities

[Have Learners (1) make word cards for words in pattern (listed on card in back of text); (2) do integrated workbook activities; (3) see additional "Suggested Activities" at end of text.]

In the morning **Wu Lei** found the boy sleeping in the garden. He woke him gently.

"So, young man, have you found your answer yet?"

"Yes," said the boy with a smile, "I have and I am no longer troubled."

"Good," said **Wu Lei** and began weeding his garden. The boy knelt down beside him and they weeded together, talking all the while of nature and life. And that is where the boy could be found each Sunday **thereafter.**

/huge, sorts, food, though, yard, feed, large, morning, gently, yes, weeding, weeded, Sunday/

Unit 49

Setting the Context

Tutor/Learners—[Introduce/ask about/discuss the topic. Learners read title, look at illustration. (Discuss) Give positive response. Read whole chapter by sentences, phrases, finger sliding under words. Learners follow silently.]

Vocabulary occasionally, shadows, licked

Tutor/Learners—[Read Unit 49, the "Conclusion". Learners follow silently; Learners then read aloud with you (echo reading). Continue to slide finger under words each time you read a selection.]

Tutor—[Work with one vocabulary word at a time; say the word as you write it.] Copy this vocabulary word, **occasionally**, on a 3 x 5 card. Find the word in the story and read the sentence with me. What do you think **occasionally** might mean? [Accept tentative definitions. If none is correct, refer Learners to dictionary. Discuss which definition is most appropriate to the context. Restate the definition in the group's own words.]

Get your vocabulary card for **occasionally**. On the back of the card, write the definition of the word. Write a sentence using the word **occasionally**.

[Repeat this procedure for each of the vocabulary words.]

Sight Words /silently, occasionally, visible, flames, whose, flickering, shadows, licked, shadowy, beyond, fleeting, sure/

Tutor/Learners—[Re-read Unit 49, Learners follow silently; Learners then read aloud with you (echo reading). Then read sight words, pointing to each word as you say it. Learners copy words on word cards, saying each one as it is written.

Teach sight words as previously shown: review/mix the order of the cards/add word cards of previously learned words/make sentences with cards such as: **Silently the flames flickered through the forest.**]

Conclusion

Unit 49

Parents **gathered** up their **tired** and **sleepy** children, silently carrying them to their beds. Occasionally, a **weary** parent **glanced** back at the fire. The old woman was **barely** visible, sitting there **beyond** the flames whose flickering shadows licked at her face. Her **shape** became more and more shadowy as the parents got **farther** from the fire, until they could not be sure if she was still there at all.

Pattern /-ure/

Tutor—[Teach words in the **-ure** pattern as in **sure.**] Get your word card for **sure** and read it. If this word is **sure**, what is this word? (**cure**)

[As you speak, write the word. Wait for Learner's response. Have Learners suggest new words, discuss meanings, add to list. Have Learners write pattern and patterned words in their notebooks.]

End of Chapter Assisted Reading

Tutor—[Read the unit first, Learners following silently. Then read it together (echo reading). Read a third time; Learners read the words they know, you read the others (shared reading).]

End of Chapter Assisted Reading

(1) Read chapter to Learners
(2) Read chapter with Learners [echo reading]
(3) Read chapter with Learners [shared reading]

End of Chapter Activities

[Have Learners (1) make word cards for words in pattern (listed on card in back of text); (2) do integrated workbook activities; (3) see additional "Suggested Activities" at end of text.]

When the parents stopped to peer into the darkness **surrounding** *the glow of the fire, she was gone. The only* **movement** *beyond the fire was far up in the heavens, where a* **shooting** *star* **sparked briefly** *and* **trailed** *its fleeting flame across the clear night sky.*

/silently, occasionally, visible, flames, whose, flickering, shadows, licked, shadowy, beyond, fleeting, sure/

Unit 50

Setting the Context

Tutor—You have just been reading folktales from many lands, stories handed down through the generations. Which one did you like best? [Wait for Learners' responses] What did you particularly like about the story? [Wait for Learners' responses. Discuss, respond positively.]

Today you have an opportunity to write your own folktale. It might be a story that your family tells. It might be a story about someone in your family who did something exciting or funny or frightening. Perhaps a member of your family came from another country and has told you a story of that country. It could be about a "haunted" house on the street where you grew up or a mysterious person who lives in your neighborhood. Perhaps you have a story within yourself that you'd like to write about. Use your imagination and write your own folktale!

Instructions for Writing

Tutor—First, think about what you want to write. List the ideas you want to write about/list the words you want to use/think about writing a surprise or "twist" ending. [Remind Learners of the suprise endings in "The Coyote and the Cowboy" and "The House of Her Dreams".] In your writing, remember the five W's—**who, why, what, when and where**.

Write the story/re-read it/make changes until it says more clearly what you want it to say/read it to others/ask for suggestions/re-write it once more/share it with us!

Most of the stories you have been reading in this book were made up a long time ago and told over and over again before they were ever **written** down. However, one of them was **written** just for this book. It was **written** in the **style** of a **folktale.**

In this **unit,** you are asked to write a **folktale.** Maybe you have a funny story about a "**character**" in your family. Maybe you have a story about the first **members** of your family to come to North **America.** Maybe you just have a story **within** that you want to tell others. Now is your **chance.** Write a story to **share** with someone else.

Suggested Activities

1. Reread earlier chapters (units) of the current story.

2. Have Learner(s) circle all instances of a given word in a newspaper article.

3. Make *Bingo* boards with word squares to match the word cards. Scatter word cards on the table face down. Turn up a card. If it matches a word square on a player's board, the player pronounces the words and puts the card over the word square on the board. A full row vertically, horizontally or diagonally wins.

4. Have Learner(s) make new sentences or phrases with the word cards they have accumulated. Use blank cards for the words they need to make a complete sentence or phrase but have not studied yet. This practice points up the need for the function words such as: *and, but, the, while, after, before*. This will also expand their learning into less structured, yet needed areas of interest (job terms, family names, current interests).

5. Ask your Learner(s) to supply a *synonym* (a word the same as) or an *antonym* (a word the opposite of) for each of the words on the list or have your Learner(s) use the words in sentences.

6. Cut apart a comic strip. Have your Learner(s) reassemble the sections correctly or suggest what might be in the speech balloons. Go on a field trip with your Learner(s) related to *Read On! II* stories.

7. Read a news story. Answer the questions: Who, What, When, Where, Why and How.

8. Have Learner(s) do investigative work at the local library. Relate to *Read On! II* stories, e.g.,

   a. Learner(s) could search for other folktales, or oral histories.

   b. Find other books about music or musicians. Look for song books, or record albums with lyrics printed on back cover. (William Graves, *How to Teach Adults*, 1984)

9. *Writing Activities.* Encourage learners to write from the first lessons:

   a. Write a Language Experience Story based on the discussion questions at the beginning of each chapter in *Read On! II*. Have learners write the letters they can in a word, using a dash for the letters they do not know. Write final version on charts. Hang charts on wall for free reading.

   b. Make lists of words relative to the same topic: medicine—doctor, pill, hospital, operation, insurance; kitchen—cook, pots, pans, stove. Draw charts of the words with the topic in a center circle and the words on lines reaching out from the circle's boundaries. Group branching lines according to learners' judgments as to "most alike" vs "not quite alike."

Scope and Sequence Book 5

	Sight Words		Patterns		Phonics
Unit 42	story	dark	mean	low	
	dark	mark	meaning	glow	
	glowing	remark	lean	slow	
	peer	remarkable	clean	blow	
	outward	shark	jean	row	
	meaning	park		grow	
	throat	spark		throw	
	humor			snow	
	always			know	
	stories			show	
	heart			tow	
	believe				
	ourselves				
Unit 43A	both	fact	biggest	self	
	Africa	factor	finest	myself	
	river	factory	happiest	yourself	
	debts	act	cleanest	himself	
	much	actor	darkest	herself	
	richest	action		itself	
	fact			ourselves	
	himself			yourselves	
	collector			themselves	
Unit 43B	debtor			actor	
	owe			collector	
	also			debtor	
	collect			doctor	
	argument			director	
	followed			sailor	
	beside				
	argued				
	contest				

	Sight Words	**Patterns**		**Phonics**
Unit 44	island	I'll	beak	vine
	decided	you'll	weak	wine
	leave	he'll	peak	whine
	I'll	she'll	speak	diner
	mouth	it'll	leak	fine
	ocean	we'll		
	agreed	you'll		
	eagerly	they'll		
	beak			clearly
	toward			happily
	sea			strongly
	goodbye			darkly
	noticed			surely
	vine			
	surely			
Unit 45A	justice	give	cry	cried
	young	live	try	tried
	adults		fry	fried
	judge		dry	dried
	lived			
	murdered			
	brought			
	crime			
	verdict			
	shall			
	repair			
	cried			
Unit 45B	self-centered		ought	
	thought		thought	
	reconsider		brought	
	however			
	those			

	Sight Words	Patterns		Phonics
		Contractions		
Unit 46A	questions	I've	I'm	we're
	United States	you've	you're	you're
	whether	he's	he's	they're
	dusty	she's	she's	
	I've	it's	it's	
	left	we've		
	famous	you've		
	you're	they've		
	I'm			
	you've			
	really			
	dare			
	Little			
	Partner			
	medicine			
Unit 46B	chance	mount		borrower
	trickster	mountain		buyer
	idea	fountain		seller
	borrow	count		lender
	horse	county		teacher
	easily			
	hardly			
	fortune	borrow		trickster
	opposite	tomorrow		gangster
	mount	sorrow		minister
	again			teamster
Unit 46C	perhaps	belt	nice	dusty
	disguise	felt	rice	shiny
	jacket	melt	price	leaky
	allow	knelt	lice	showy
	secretly		slice	
	jabbing		dice	
	shiny		mice	
	boots		spice	
	belt			
	sadly			
	pants			
	short			
	nice			

	Sight Words		**Patterns**		**Phonics**
Unit 47A	house	range		forward	
	dreams	strange		backward	
	strange	change		outward	
	ghost	arrange		inward	
	breakfast			upward	
	husband			downward	
	ever			toward	
	warm				
	garden				
	exist				
	afterwards				
	family				
	forward				
Unit 47B	real estate		real		own
	quite		seal		shown
	front		steal		known
	shown		heal		grown
	stranger		meal		mown
	property				
	quickly				
	couple				
	sign				
	entering				
	bother				
	none				
Unit 48A	boy	boy	rang	careful	
	carefully	joy	sang	carefully	
	careful	toy	bang	hopeful	
	says	Roy	hang		
	farmers	royal			
	head				
	held				
	nose				
	soups				
	together				
	rang				

	Sight Words	**Patterns**	**Phonics**
Unit 48B	troubling	burn	
	son	turn	
	troubled		
	become		
	learned		
	Heaven		
	burn		
	true		
	robe		
Unit 48C	huge	weed	yard
	sorts	feed	hard
	food	need	card
	though	needle	lard
	yard		hardly
	feed		
	large		
	morning		
	gently		
	yes		
	weeding		
	weeded		
	Sunday		
Unit 49	silently		sure
	occasionally		cure
	visible		pure
	flames		lure
	whose		
	flickering		
	shadows		
	licked		
	shadowy		
	beyond		
	fleeting		
	sure		

Cut out word cards along dotted lines.

Unit 42

story	dark	mean	low
dark	mark	meaning	glow
glowing	remark	lean	slow
peer	remarkable	clean	blow
outward	shark	jean	row
meaning	park		grow
throat	spark		throw
humor			snow
always			know
stories			show
heart			tow
believe			
ourselves			

Unit 43A

both	fact	biggest	self
Africa	factor	finest	myself
river	factory	happiest	yourself
debts	act	cleanest	himself
much	actor	darkest	herself
richest	action		itself
fact			ourselves
himself			yourselves
collector			themselves

Unit 43B

debtor	actor
owe	collector
also	debtor
collect	doctor
argument	director
followed	sailor
beside	
argued	
contest	

Unit 44

island	I'll	beak	vine	clearly
decided	you'll	weak	wine	happily
leave	he'll	peak	whine	strongly
I'll	she'll	speak	diner	darkly
mouth	it'll	leak	fine	surely
ocean	we'll			
agreed	you'll			
eagerly	they'll			
beak				
toward				
sea				
goodbye				
noticed				
vine				
surely				

Cut out word cards along dotted lines.

Unit 45A

give	cry	cried
live	try	tried
	fry	fried
	dry	dried

justice
young
adults
judge
lived
murdered
brought
crime
verdict
shall
repair
cried

Unit 45B

self-centered	ought
thought	thought
reconsider	brought
however	
those	

Unit 46A

questions
United States
whether
dusty
I've
left
famous
you're
I'm
you've
really

dare
Little
Partner
medicine

Contractions

I've	I'm
you've	you're
he's	he's
she's	she's
it's	it's
we've	we're
you've	you're
they've	they're

Unit 46B

chance
trickster
idea
borrow
horse
easily
hardly
fortune
opposite
mount
again

mount	borrower
mountain	buyer
fountain	seller
count	lender
county	teacher
borrow	trickster
tomorrow	gangster
sorrow	minister
	teamster

Cut out word cards along dotted lines.

Unit 46C

belt	ice	dusty
felt	nice	shiny
melt	rice	leaky
knelt	price	showy
	lice	
	slice	
	dice	
	mice	
	spice	

perhaps
disguise
jacket
allow
secretly
jabbing
shiny
boots
belt
sadly
pants
short
nice

house
dreams
strange
ghost
breakfast
husband
ever
warm
garden
exist
afterwards
family
forward

Unit 47A

range	forward
strange	backward
change	outward
arrange	inward
	upward
	downward
	toward

Unit 47B

real	own
seal	shown
steal	known
heal	grown
meal	mown

real estate
quite
front
shown
stranger
property
quickly
couple
sign
entering
bother
none

boy
carefully
careful
says
farmers
head
held
nose
soups
together
rang

Unit 48A

boy	rang	careful
joy	sang	carefully
toy	bang	hopeful
Roy	hang	
royal		

Cut out word cards along dotted lines.

Unit 48B

troubling
son
troubled
become
learned
Heaven
burn
true
robe

burn
turn

Unit 48C

huge
sorts
food
though
yard
feed
large
morning
gently
yes
weeding
weeded
Sunday

weed
feed
need
needle

yard
hard
card
lard
hardly

Unit 49

silently
occasionally
visible
flames
whose
flickering
shadows
licked
shadowy
beyond
fleeting
sure

sure
cure
pure
lure